Christmas Friends

by Linda A. Daley

LEISURE ARTS, INC. • Maumelle, Arkansas

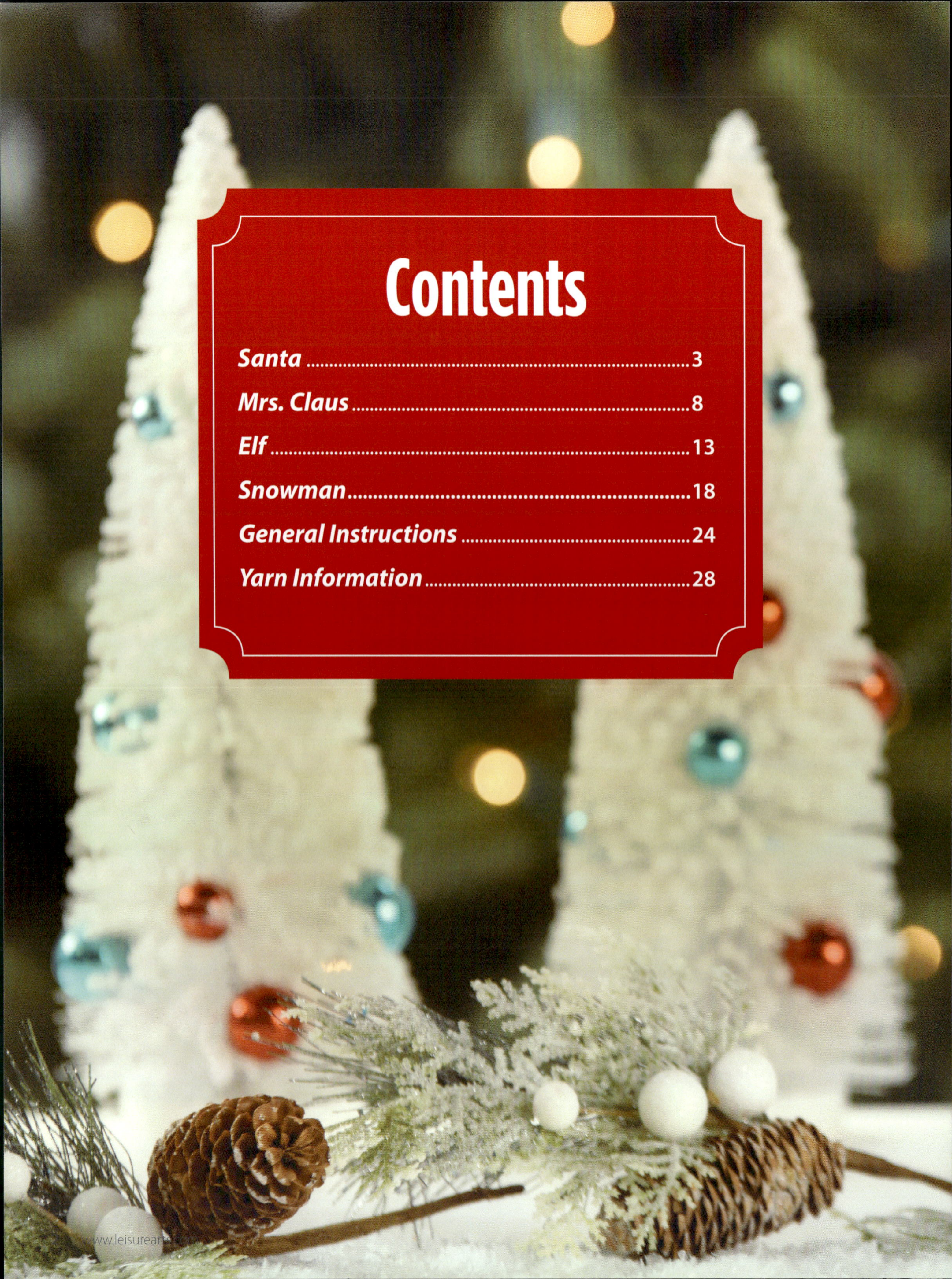

Contents

Santa

EASY

Finished Size: 8" (20.5 cm) tall

SHOPPING LIST

Yarn (Medium Weight) 4

- ☐ Red - 45 yards (41 meters)
- ☐ White - 25 yards (23 meters)
- ☐ Black - 22 yards (20 meters)
- ☐ Lt Pink - 21 yards (19 meters)
- ☐ Green - 5 yards (4.5 meters)

Crochet Hook

- ☐ Size G (4 mm)

  or size needed for gauge

Additional Supplies

- ☐ Polyester fiberfill
- ☐ Yarn needle

GAUGE INFORMATION

8 sc and 8 rows/rnds = 2" (5 cm)

Gauge Swatch: 2" (5 cm) square

Ch 9.

Row 1: Sc in second ch from hook and in each ch across: 8 sc.

Rows 2-8: Ch 1, turn; sc in each sc across.

Finish off.

STITCH GUIDE

SINGLE CROCHET 2 TOGETHER

(abbreviated sc2tog)

Pull up a loop in each of next 2 sts, YO and draw through all 3 loops on hook **(counts as one sc)**.

Head & Body

Rnd 1 (Right side)**:** With Lt Pink, ch 2, 6 sc in second ch from hook; do **not** join, place marker to indicated the beginning of the rnd ***(see Markers, page 25)***.

Note: Loop a short piece of yarn around any stitch to mark Rnd 1 as **right** side.

Rnd 2: 2 Sc in each sc around: 12 sc.

Rnd 3: (2 Sc in next sc, sc in next sc) around: 18 sc.

Rnd 4: (2 Sc in next sc, sc in next 2 sc) around: 24 sc.

Rnd 5: (2 Sc in next sc, sc in next 3 sc) around: 30 sc.

Rnds 6-11: Sc in each sc around.

Rnd 12: (Sc2tog, sc in next 4 sc) around: 25 sc.

Rnd 13: Sc in each sc around.

Rnd 14: (Sc2tog, sc in next 3 sc) around: 20 sc.

Rnd 15: (Sc2tog, sc in next 2 sc) around: 15 sc.

Rnd 16: (Sc2tog, sc in next sc) around, changing to Red in last sc ***(Fig. 4b, page 26)***; cut Lt Pink: 10 sc:

Stuff Head with polyester fiberfill.

Rnd 17: 2 Sc in each sc around: 20 sc.

Rnd 18: Sc in each sc around.

Rnd 19: (2 Sc in next sc, sc in next sc) around: 30 sc.

Rnds 20 and 21: Sc in each sc around.

Rnd 22: (2 Sc in next sc, sc in next 4 sc) around: 36 sc.

Rnd 23: Sc in each sc around.

Rnd 24: (2 Sc in next sc, sc in next 5 sc) around: 42 sc.

Rnds 25 and 26: Sc in each sc around, changing to Black in last sc of Rnd 26; drop Red to **wrong** side of work.

Rnd 27 (Belt)**:** Hdc in next sc and in each sc around changing to Red in last hdc; cut Black.

Rnd 28: Working in Back Loops Only ***(Fig. 2, page 26)***, (sc2tog, sc in next 4 sc) around: 35 sc.

Rnd 29: Working in both loops, (sc2tog, sc in next 3 sc) around: 28 sc.

Rnd 30: (Sc2tog, sc in next 2 sc) around: 21 sc.

Rnd 31: (Sc2tog, sc in next sc) around: 14 sc.

Stuff Body with polyester fiberfill.

Rnd 32: Sc2tog around; slip st in next sc, finish off leaving a 6" (15 cm) length for sewing.

Thread yarn needle with end and weave yarn through Front Loops Only of remaining sc ***(Fig. 2, page 26)***; secure end.

TRIM

Rnd 1: With **right** side facing, Head toward you, and working in free loops of hdc on Rnd 27 ***(Fig. 3a, page 26)***, join White with sc in first hdc ***(see Joining With Sc, page 25)***; sc in each st around; join with slip st to first sc: 42 sc.

Rnd 2: Ch 1, sc in same st as joining and in each sc around; join with slip st to first sc, finish off.

Boot & Leg (Make 2)

With Black, ch 5.

Rnd 1 (Right side)**:** Sc in second ch from hook and in next 2 chs, 5 sc in last ch; working in free loops of beginning ch ***(Fig. 3b, page 26)***, sc in next 2 chs, 2 sc in next ch; join with slip st to first sc: 12 sc.

Note: Mark Rnd 1 as **right** side.

Rnd 2: Ch 1, sc in same st as joining and in next 2 sc, 2 sc in next sc, sc in next sc, 3 sc in next sc, sc in next sc, 2 sc in next sc, sc in next 3 sc, 3 sc in last sc; join with slip st in first sc: 18 sc.

Rnd 3: Ch 1, sc in same st as joining and in next 3 sc, 2 sc in next sc, (sc in next sc, 2 sc in next sc) 3 times, sc in next 5 sc, 3 sc in next sc, sc in last sc; join with slip st to Back Loop Only of first sc: 24 sc.

Rnd 4 (Sole ridge)**:** Ch 1, sc in same st as joining and in Back Loop Only of each sc around; join with slip st to **both** loops of first sc.

Rnd 5: Ch 1, sc in same st as joining and in both loops of each sc around; join with slip st to first sc.

Rnd 6: Ch 1, sc in same st as joining and in next 5 sc, sc2tog 5 times, sc in last 8 sc; join with slip st to first sc: 19 sc.

Rnd 7: Ch 1, sc in same st as joining and in next 4 sc, sc2tog 3 times, sc in last 8 sc; join with slip st to first sc: 16 sc.

Rnd 8: Ch 1, sc in same st as joining and in next 4 sc, sc2tog twice, sc in last 7 sc; join with slip st to first sc changing to White ***(Fig. 4a, page 26)***; cut Black: 14 sc.

Rnd 9: Ch 1, sc in same st as joining and in each sc around; join with slip st to first sc.

Stuff Foot with polyester fiberfill.

Rnd 10: Ch 1, sc in same st as joining and in each sc around; join with slip st to first sc changing to Red; cut White.

Rnd 11: Ch 1, sc in same st as joining and in each sc around; join with slip st to first sc, finish off leaving a 10" (25.5 cm) length for sewing.

Stuff Leg firmly with polyester fiberfill.

Mitt & Arm (Make 2)

Rnd 1 (Right side)**:** With Green, ch 2; 5 sc in second ch from hook; do **not** join, place marker to indicate the beginning of the rnd.

Note: Mark Rnd 1 as **right** side.

Rnd 2: 2 Sc in each sc around: 10 sc.

Rnd 3: (Sc in next 4 sc, 2 sc in next sc) twice: 12 sc.

Rnd 4: Sc in each sc around; slip st in next sc, finish off.

Rnd 5: With **right** side facing, join White with sc in same st as slip st; sc in each sc around; join with slip st to first sc.

Rnd 6: Ch 1, sc in same st as joining and in each sc around; join with slip st to first sc, finish off.

Rnd 7: With **right** side facing, join Red with sc in same st as joining; sc in each sc around; join with slip st to first sc.

Rnd 8: Ch 1, sc in same st as joining and in each sc around; do **not** join, place marker to indicate the beginning of the rnd.

Rnds 9-11: Sc in each sc around.

Rnd 12: (Sc2tog, sc in next 4 sc) twice: 10 sc.

Stuff Arm with polyester fiberfill.

Joining Row: Ch 1; flatten top of Arm having ch at fold. Working through **both** loops of **both** pieces, sc in each st across; finish off leaving an 8" (20.5 cm) length for sewing.

Cap

BRIM

With White, ch 34; being careful **not** to twist ch, join with slip st to first ch to form a ring.

Rnd 1 (Right side)**:** Ch 1, sc in same ch as joining and in each ch around; join with slip st to first sc.

Note: Mark Rnd 1 as **right** side.

Rnd 2: Ch 1, sc in same st as joining and in each sc around; join with slip st to first sc, finish off.

BODY

Rnd 1: With **right** side facing and working in free loops of beginning ch, join Red with sc in first st; sc in each st around; join with slip st to first sc: 34 sc.

Note: Mark Rnd 1 as **right** side.

Rnd 2: Ch 1, sc in same st as joining, ★ sc2tog, sc in next 4 sc, sc2tog, sc in next 3 sc; repeat from ★ 2 times **more**; do **not** join, place marker to indicate the beginning of the rnd: 28 sc.

Rnd 3: (Sc2tog, sc in next 5 sc) around: 24 sc.

Rnd 4: Sc in each sc around.

Rnd 5: (Sc2tog, sc in next 4 sc) around: 20 sc.

Rnd 6: (Sc2tog, sc in next 3 sc) around: 16 sc.

Rnd 7: Sc in each sc around.

Begin working in rows.

Row 8: Ch 1; flatten top of Body having ch at fold. Working through **both** loops of **both** pieces, sc in each st across: 8 sc.

Row 9: Ch 1, turn; sc in each sc across.

Rows 10-15: Ch 1, turn; beginning in first sc, sc2tog, sc in each sc across: 2 sc.

Row 16: Ch 1, turn; beginning in first sc, sc2tog: one sc.

Row 17: Ch 1, turn; sc in sc; finish off.

POM-POM

Rnd 1 (Right side)**:** With White, make an adjustable ring and work 5 sc in ring ***(Figs. 1a-d, page 25)***; do **not** join, place marker to indicated the beginning of the rnd.

Note: Mark Rnd 1 as **right** side.

Rnd 2: 2 Sc in each sc around: 10 sc.

Rnd 3: Sc in each sc around.

Rnd 4: Sc2tog 5 times; slip st in next sc, finish off leaving a 6" (15 cm) length for sewing.

Stuff piece lightly with polyester fiberfill.

Thread yarn needle with end and weave yarn through Front Loops Only of remaining sc; secure end, then sew to last sc on Row 17 of Cap.

Beard

With White, ch 15.

Row 1: Slip st in second ch from hook and in next 5 chs, ch 3 (mouth opening), skip next 2 chs, slip st in last 6 chs: 12 slip sts and one ch-3 sp.

Row 2 (Right side)**:** Ch 1, turn; sc in first 2 slip sts, ch 3, (sc in next slip st, ch 3) 4 times, (sc, ch 3) 3 times in next ch-3 sp, (sc in next slip st, ch 3) 4 times, sc in last 2 slip sts: 15 sc and 12 ch-3 sps.

Note: Mark Row 2 as **right** side.

Row 3: Ch 1, turn; sc in first 2 sc, skip next ch-3 sp, (sc in next sc keeping ch-3 to **right** side of work, skip next ch-3 sp) 11 times, sc in last 2 sc keeping ch-3 to **right** side of work: 15 sc.

Row 4: Ch 1, turn; slip st in first 3 sc, ch 4, (sc in next sc, ch 4) 3 times, (sc, ch 4) twice in next sc, sc in next sc, ch 4, (sc, ch 4) twice in next sc, (sc in next sc, ch 4) 3 times, slip st in next sc, leave remaining 2 sc unworked: 11 sc and 12 ch-4 sps.

Row 5: Ch 1, turn; skip first ch-4 sp, (sc in next sc keeping ch-4 to **right** side of work, skip next ch-4 sp) 11 times, slip st in next slip st keeping ch-4 to **right** side of work: 11 sc.

Row 6: Ch 1, turn; skip first slip st, slip st in next 3 sc, ch 4, sc in next sc, ch 4, ★ (sc, ch 4) twice in next sc, sc in next sc, ch 4; repeat from ★ once **more**, slip st in next sc, leave remaining 2 sc unworked: 7 sc and 8 ch-4 sps.

Row 7: Ch 1, turn; skip first ch-4 sp, (sc in next sc keeping ch-4 to **right** side of work, skip next ch-4 sp) 7 times, slip st in next slip st keeping ch-4 to **right** side of work; finish off.

Nose

With Lt Pink, ch 2, YO, insert hook in second ch from hook, YO and pull up a loop, YO, insert hook in **same** ch, YO and pull up a loop (5 loops on hook), YO and draw through all 5 loops on hook, ch 2, slip st in same ch; finish off leaving an 8" (20.5 cm) length for sewing.

Button (Make 2)

With Black, make an adjustable ring and work 5 sc in ring; join with slip st to first sc; finish off leaving a 6" (15 cm) length for sewing.

Finishing

Using Photo as a guide for placement and long ends:

- On Rnds 9 and 10, sew Nose to center of face.
- With Black and using overcast stitch, add eyes on Rnd 8 ***(Fig. 8, page 27)*** leaving 3 stitches between eyes.
- With Red, add straight stitch mouth between Rnds 11 and 12 ***(Fig. 7, page 27)***, centering below Nose.
- Sew one Arm to each side of Body.
- Sew Legs to Body.
- Sew Buttons to center of Body.
- Sew Beard to facing having mouth opening over Red mouth; sew Hat to Head overlapping each side of Beard.

Mrs. Claus

EASY

Finished Size: 8" (20.5 cm) tall

SHOPPING LIST

Yarn (Medium Weight) 4

- ☐ Red - 54 yards (49.5 meters)
- ☐ White - 43 yards (39.5 meters)
- ☐ Lt Pink - 25 yards (23 meters)
- ☐ Black - 17 yards (15.5 meters)
- ☐ Green - small amount

Crochet Hook

- ☐ Size G (4 mm)
  or size needed for gauge

Additional Supplies

- ☐ Polyester fiberfill
- ☐ Yarn needle

GAUGE INFORMATION

8 sc and 8 rows/rnds = 2" (5 cm)

Gauge Swatch: 2" (5 cm) square

Ch 9.

Row 1: Sc in second ch from hook and in each ch across: 8 sc.

Rows 2-8: Ch 1, turn; sc in each sc across.

Finish off.

STITCH GUIDE

SINGLE CROCHET 2 TOGETHER

(abbreviated sc2tog)

Pull up a loop in each of next 2 sts, YO and draw through all 3 loops on hook **(counts as one sc)**.

Head & Body

Rnd 1 (Right side)**:** With Lt Pink, ch 2, 6 sc in second ch from hook; do **not** join, place marker to indicated the beginning of the rnd ***(see Markers, page 25)***.

Note: Loop a short piece of yarn around any stitch to mark Rnd 1 as **right** side.

Rnd 2: 2 Sc in each sc around: 12 sc.

Rnd 3: (2 Sc in next sc, sc in next sc) around: 18 sc.

Rnd 4: (2 Sc in next sc, sc in next 2 sc) around: 24 sc.

Rnd 5: (2 Sc in next sc, sc in next 3 sc) around: 30 sc.

Rnds 6-11: Sc in each sc around.

Rnd 12: (Sc2tog, sc in next 4 sc) around: 25 sc.

Rnd 13: Sc in each sc around.

Rnd 14: (Sc2tog, sc in next 3 sc) around: 20 sc.

Rnd 15: (Sc2tog, sc in next 2 sc) around: 15 sc.

Rnd 16: (Sc2tog, sc in next sc) around changing to Red in last sc ***(Fig. 4b, page 26)***; cut Lt Pink: 10 sc.

Stuff Head with polyester fiberfill.

Rnd 17: 2 Sc in each sc around: 20 sc.

Rnd 18: Sc in each sc around.

Rnd 19: (2 Sc in next sc, sc in next sc) around: 30 sc.

Rnd 20: Sc in each sc around.

Rnd 21: (2 Sc in next sc, sc in next 4 sc) around: 36 sc.

Rnd 22: Sc in each sc around.

Rnd 23: (Sc2tog, sc in next 2 sc) around changing to White in last sc made, drop Red to **wrong** side of work: 27 sc.

Rnd 24 (Apron tie)**:** With White, sc in each sc around changing to Red in last sc; cut White.

Rnd 25: Working in Back Loops Only ***(Fig. 2, page 26)***, (2 sc in next sc, sc in next 2 sc) around: 36 sc.

Rnd 26: Sc in each sc around.

Rnd 27: (2 Sc in next sc, sc in next 5 sc) around: 42 sc.

Rnds 28 and 29: Sc in each sc around.

Rnd 30: Working in Back Loops Only, (sc2tog, sc in next 4 sc) around: 35 sc.

Rnd 31: (Sc2tog, sc in next 3 sc) around: 28 sc.

Rnd 32: (Sc2tog, sc in next 2 sc) around: 21 sc.

Rnd 33: (Sc2tog, sc in next sc) around: 14 sc.

Stuff Body with polyester fiberfill.

Rnd 34: Sc2tog around; slip st in next sc, finish off leaving a 6" (15 cm) length for sewing.

Thread yarn needle with end and weave yarn through Front Loops Only of remaining sc ***(Fig. 2, page 26)***; secure end.

SKIRT

Rnd 1: With right **side** facing, Head toward you, and working in free loops of sc on Rnd 29 ***(Fig. 3a, page 26)***, join Red with sc in first st ***(see Joining With Sc, page 25)***; sc in each st around; join with slip st to first sc: 42 sc.

Rnds 2-4: Ch 1, sc in same st as joining and in each sc around; join with slip st to first sc.

Rnd 5: Ch 1, hdc in same st as joining and in each sc around; join with slip st to first hdc, finish off.

Rnd 6 (Ruffle)**:** With **right** side facing and Head toward you, join White with slip st in same st as joining; ch 1, (slip st in next hdc, ch 1) around; join with slip st to first slip st, finish off.

Boot & Leg (Make 2)

With Black, ch 5.

Rnd 1 (Right side)**:** Sc in second ch from hook and in next 2 chs, 5 sc in last ch; working in free loops of beginning ch ***(Fig. 3b, page 26)***, sc in next 2 chs, 2 sc in next ch; join with slip st to first sc: 12 sc.

Note: Mark Rnd 1 as **right** side.

Rnd 2: Ch 1, sc in same st as joining and in next 2 sc, 2 sc in next sc, sc in next sc, 3 sc in next sc, sc in next sc, 2 sc in next sc, sc in next 3 sc, 3 sc in last sc; join with slip st in first sc: 18 sc.

Rnd 3: Ch 1, sc in same st as joining and in next 3 sc, 2 sc in next sc, (sc in next sc, 2 sc in next sc) 3 times, sc in next 5 sc, 3 sc in next sc, sc in last sc; join with slip st to Back Loop Only of first sc: 24 sc.

Rnd 4 (Sole ridge)**:** Ch 1, sc in same st as joining and in Back Loop Only of each sc around; join with slip st to **both** loops of first sc.

Rnd 5: Ch 1, sc in same st as joining and in both loops of each sc around; join with slip st to first sc.

Rnd 6: Ch 1, sc in same st as joining and in next 5 sc, sc2tog 5 times, sc in last 8 sc; join with slip st to first sc: 19 sc.

Rnd 7: Ch 1, sc in same st as joining and in next 4 sc, sc2tog 3 times, sc in last 8 sc; join with slip st to first sc, changing to White ***(Fig. 4a, page 26)***; cut Black: 16 sc.

Rnd 8: Ch 1, sc in same st as joining and in next 4 sc, sc2tog twice, sc in last 7 sc; join with slip st to first sc: 14 sc.

Rnds 9 and 10: Ch 1, sc in same st as joining and in each sc around; join with slip st to first sc, at end of Rnd 10, finish off leaving a 10" (25.5 cm) length for sewing.

Stuff Leg with polyester fiberfill.

Hand & Arm (Make 2)

Rnd 1 (Right side)**:** With Lt Pink, ch 2; 5 sc in second ch from hook; do **not** join, place marker to indicate the beginning of the rnd.

Note: Mark Rnd 1 as **right** side.

Rnd 2: 2 Sc in each sc around: 10 sc.

Rnd 3: (Sc in next 4 sc, 2 sc in next sc) twice: 12 sc.

Rnd 4: Sc in each sc around; slip st in Back Loop Only of next sc changing to Red; cut Lt Pink.

Rnd 5: Ch 1, sc in same st as slip st and in Back Loop Ony of each sc around; join with slip st to **both** loops of first sc.

Rnd 6: Ch 1, sc in same st as joining and in both loops of each sc around; do **not** join, place marker to indicate the beginning of the rnd.

Rnds 7-11: Sc in each sc around.

Rnd 12: (Sc2tog, sc in next 4 sc) twice: 10 sc.

Stuff Arm with polyester fiberfill.

Joining Row: Ch 1; flatten top of Arm having ch at fold. Working through **both** loops of **both** pieces, sc in each st across; finish off leaving an 8" (20.5 cm) length for sewing.

Trim: With **right** side facing, Hand toward you and working in free loops of sc on Rnd 4, join White with slip st in first st; ch 1, (slip st in next st, ch 1) around; join with slip st to first slip st, finish off.

Apron

Row 1 (Right side)**:** With White, ch 4; sc in second ch from hook and in next ch, 4 sc in last ch; working in free loops of beginning ch, sc in next 2 chs; do **not** join: 8 sc.

Note: Mark Row 1 as **right** side.

Row 2: Ch 2 (does **not** count as a st), turn; dc in first sc, hdc in next 2 sc, 2 sc in each of next 2 sc, hdc in next 2 sc, dc in last sc: 10 sts.

Row 3: Ch 2 (does **not** count as a st), turn; hdc in first 2 sts, 2 hdc in next hdc, hdc in next sc, 2 sc in each of next 2 sc, hdc in next sc, 2 hdc in next hdc, hdc in next hdc, 2 hdc in last dc: 15 sts.

Edging Rnd: Ch 1, do **not** turn; work 8 sc evenly spaced across end of rows, ch 1; working in sts on Row 3, (slip st in next st, ch 1) across; join with slip st to first sc, finish off leaving an 8" (20.5 cm) length for sewing.

Using 2 plies of each color, add Red French Knot berries ***(Fig. 5, page 27)*** and Green straight stitch leaves ***(Fig. 7, page 27)*** to **right** side of Apron using photo as a guide for placement.

Hair

Rnd 1 (Right side)**:** With White, make an adjustable ring, ch 1 and work 8 hdc in ring ***(Figs. 1a-d, page 25)***; join with slip st to first hdc: 8 hdc.

Note: Mark Rnd 1 as **right** side.

Rnd 2: Ch 1, 2 hdc in same st as joining and in each hdc around; join with slip st to first hdc: 16 hdc.

Rnd 3: Ch 1, sc in same st as joining and in each hdc around; join with slip st to first sc.

Rnd 4: Ch 1, beginning in same st as joining, sc2tog around; join with slip st to first sc: 8 sc.

Rnd 5: Ch 1, 2 sc in same st as joining and in each sc around; join with slip st to first sc: 16 sc.

Rnd 6: Ch 1, hdc in same st as joining, 2 hdc in next sc, (hdc in next sc, 2 hdc in next sc) around; join with slip st to first hdc: 24 hdc.

Rnd 7: Ch 1, hdc in same st as joining and in next hdc, 2 hdc in next hdc, (hdc in next 2 hdc, 2 hdc in next hdc) around; join with slip st to first hdc: 32 hdc.

Rnds 8 and 9: Ch 1, hdc in same st as joining and in each hdc around; join with slip st to first hdc.

Rnd 10: Ch 1, sc in same st as joining, sc2tog, sc in next hdc, sc2tog, sc in next 3 hdc, hdc in next 3 hdc, 2 hdc in next hdc, 2 dc in next hdc, (2 dc, hdc) in next hdc, skip next hdc, slip st in next hdc, skip next hdc, (hdc, 2 dc) in next hdc, 2 dc in next hdc, 2 hdc in next hdc, hdc in next 3 hdc, sc in next 3 hdc, sc2tog, sc in next hdc, sc2tog; join with slip st to first sc: 34 sts.

Rnd 11: Ch 1, sc in same st as joining and in next 3 sc, ch 1, (slip st in next st, ch 1) 12 times, slip st in next dc, skip next slip st, slip st in next dc, ch 1, (slip st in next st, ch 1) 11 times, sc in last 4 sc; join with slip st to first sc; finish off leaving a 12" (30.5 cm) length for sewing.

BUN WREATH

Foundation Ch: With White, ch 16; being careful **not** to twist ch, join with slip st to form a ring.

Candy Cane Rnd: Ch 1, sc in same ch as joining, ch 2, drop White loop from hook; with same side of Foundation Ch facing, join Red with sc in next Foundation Ch, ch 2, drop Red loop from hook; ★ insert hook in White dropped loop, keeping Red ch and working yarn **toward** you, sc in next Foundation Ch, ch 2, drop White loop from hook; insert hook in Red dropped loop, keeping White ch and working yarn **toward** you, sc in next Foundation Ch, ch 2, drop Red loop from hook; repeat from ★ 5 times **more**, insert hook in White dropped loop, keeping Red ch and work yarn **toward** you, join with slip st to first White sc, finish off White; insert hook in Red dropped loop, working **behind** first White ch-2, join with slip st to Red joining sc, finish off.

Collar

With White, ch 11.

Rnd 1 (Right side)**:** Slip st in second ch from hook, sc in next ch, hdc in next ch, 2 dc in next ch, (3 dc, hdc) in next ch, slip st in next ch, (hdc, 3 dc) in next ch, 2 dc in next ch, hdc in next ch, sc in next ch, slip st in next ch; finish off leaving a 6" (15 cm) length for sewing.

Finishing

Using Photo as a guide for placement and long ends:

- With Pink and using satin stitch ***(Fig. 6, page 27)***, add nose on Rnd 10.
- With a double strand of Black, add French knot eyes between Rnds 8 and 9.
- With Black, add an overstitch mouth on Rnd 12 ***(Fig. 8, page 27)***.
- Insert Hair Bun through Bun Wreath having wreath around Rnd 4; sew Hair to head, centering part to center of face.
- Sew one Arm to each side of Body.
- Sew Legs to Body.

Thread yarn needle with Apron end. Centering **wrong** side of Apron against **right** side of Body, sew sc to free loops of Apron tie on Rnd 24.

Elf

EASY

Finished Size: 8" (20.5 cm) tall

SHOPPING LIST

Yarn (Medium Weight) 4

- ☐ Bright Green - 38 yards (34.5 meters)
- ☐ Red - 38 yards (34.5 meters)
- ☐ Lt Pink - 27 yards (24.5 meters)
- ☐ White - 13 yards (12 meters)
- ☐ Black - 5 yards (4.5 meters)
- ☐ Gold - small amount

Crochet Hook

- ☐ Size G (4 mm) **or** size needed for gauge

Additional Supplies

- ☐ Polyester fiberfill
- ☐ Yarn needle

GAUGE INFORMATION

8 sc and 8 rows/rnds = 2" (5 cm)

Gauge Swatch: 2" (5 cm) square

Ch 9.

Row 1: Sc in second ch from hook and in each ch across: 8 sc.

Rows 2-8: Ch 1, turn; sc in each sc across.

Finish off.

STITCH GUIDE

SINGLE CROCHET 2 TOGETHER *(abbreviated sc2tog)*

Pull up a loop in each of next 2 sts, YO and draw through all 3 loops on hook **(counts as one sc)**.

Head & Body

Rnd 1 (Right side)**:** With Lt Pink, ch 2, 6 sc in second ch from hook; do **not** join, place marker to indicated the beginning of the rnd *(see Markers, page 25)*.

Note: Loop a short piece of yarn around any stitch to mark Rnd 1 as **right** side.

Rnd 2: 2 Sc in each sc around: 12 sc.

Rnd 3: (2 Sc in next sc, sc in next sc) around: 18 sc.

Rnd 4: (2 Sc in next sc, sc in next 2 sc) around: 24 sc.

Rnd 5: (2 Sc in next sc, sc in next 3 sc) around: 30 sc.

Rnds 6-11: Sc in each sc around.

Rnd 12: (Sc2tog, sc in next 4 sc) around: 25 sc.

Rnd 13: Sc in each sc around.

Rnd 14: (Sc2tog, sc in next 3 sc) around: 20 sc.

Rnd 15: (Sc2tog, sc in next 2 sc) around: 15 sc.

Rnd 16: (Sc2tog, sc in next sc) around changing to Bright Green in last sc *(Fig. 4b, page 26)*; cut Lt Pink: 10 sc.

Stuff Head with polyester fiberfill.

Rnd 17: 2 Sc in each sc around: 20 sc.

Rnd 18: Sc in each sc around.

Rnd 19: (2 Sc in next sc, sc in next sc) around: 30 sc.

Rnd 20: Sc in each sc around.

Rnd 21: (2 Sc in next sc, sc in next 4 sc) around: 36 sc.

Rnds 22 and 23: Sc in each sc around; at end of Rnd 23, slip st in next sc changing to Black ***(Fig. 4a, page 26)***, cut Bright Green.

Rnd 24: Ch 1, hdc in same st as joining and in each sc around; join with slip st to first hdc changing to Red, cut Black.

Rnd 25: Ch 1, sc in Back Loop Only of same st as joining and each hdc around ***(Fig. 2, page 26)***; join with slip st to **both** loops of first sc.

Rnd 26: Ch 1, sc in same st as joining and in both loops of each sc around; do **not** join, place marker to indicate the beginning of the rnd.

Rnds 27 and 28: Sc in each sc around.

Rnd 29: (Sc2tog, sc in next 4 sc) around: 30 sc.

Rnd 30: (Sc2tog, sc in next 3 sc) around: 24 sc.

Rnd 31: (Sc2tog, sc in next 2 sc) around: 18 sc.

Rnd 32: (Sc2tog, sc in next sc) around: 12 sc.

Stuff Body with polyester fiberfill.

Rnd 33: Sc2tog around; slip st in next sc, finish off leaving a 6" (15 cm) length for sewing.

Thread yarn needle with end and weave yarn through Front Loops Only of remaining sc ***(Fig. 2, page 26)***; secure end.

TRIM

Rnd 1: With **right** side facing, Head toward you, and working in free loops of hdc on Rnd 24 ***(Fig. 3a, page 26)***, join Green with sc in first sc ***(see Joining With Sc, page 25)***; sc in each st around; join with slip st to first sc: 42 sc.

Rnds 2-4: Ch 1, sc in same st as joining and in each sc around; join with slip st to first sc.

Finish off.

Shoe & Leg (Make 2)

With Bright Green, ch 5.

Rnd 1 (Right side)**:** Sc in second ch from hook and in next 2 chs, 5 sc in last ch; working in free loops of beginning ch ***(Fig. 3b, page 26)***, sc in next 2 chs, 2 sc in next ch; join with slip st to first sc: 12 sc.

Note: Mark Rnd 1 as **right** side.

Rnd 2: Ch 1, sc in same st as joining and in next 2 sc, 2 sc in next sc, sc in next sc, 3 sc in next sc, sc in next sc, 2 sc in next sc, sc in next 3 sc, 3 sc in last sc; join with slip st in first sc: 18 sc.

Rnd 3: Ch 1, sc in same st as joining and in next 3 sc, 2 sc in next sc, (sc in next sc, 2 sc in next sc) 3 times, sc in next 5 sc, 3 sc in next sc, sc in last sc; join with slip st to Back Loop Only of first sc: 24 sc.

Rnd 4 (Sole ridge)**:** Ch 1, sc in same st as joining and in Back Loop Only of each sc around; join with slip st to **both** loops of first sc.

Rnd 5: Ch 1, sc in both loops of same st as joining and in next 7 sc, (sc, hdc) in next sc, 2 dc in next sc, [ch 2, slip st in second ch from hook **(Picot made)**], 2 dc in next sc, (hdc, sc) in next sc, sc in last 12 sc; join with slip st to first sc: 28 sts and one Picot.

Rnd 6: Ch 1, sc in same st as joining and in next 5 sc, sc2tog twice, skip next 4 dc and Picot, sc2tog 3 times, sc in last 8 sc; join with slip st to first sc: 19 sc.

Rnd 7: Ch 1, sc in same st as joining and in next 4 sc, sc2tog 3 times, sc in last 8 sc changing to Red in last sc; do **not** join, place marker to indicate the beginning of the rnd; cut Bright Green: 16 sc.

Rnd 8: Sc in next 5 sc, sc2tog twice, sc in next 7 sc changing to White in last sc; drop Red to **wrong** side of work: 14 sc.

Rnd 9: Sc in each sc around changing to Red in last sc; drop White to **wrong** side of work.

Rnd 10: Sc in each sc around changing to White in last sc; drop Red to **wrong** side of work.

Rnd 11: Sc in each sc around changing to Red in last sc; cut White.

Rnd 12: Sc in each sc around; slip st in next sc, finish off leaving a 10" (25.5 cm) length for sewing.

Using Bright Green, sew the two dc on each side of the Picot together on toe of Shoe.
Stuff Shoe & Leg with polyester fiberfill.

Hand & Arm (Make 2)

Rnd 1 (Right side)**:** With Lt Pink, ch 2, 5 sc in second ch from hook; do **not** join, place marker to indicate the beginning of the rnd.

Note: Mark Rnd 1 as **right** side.

Rnd 2: 2 Sc in each sc around: 10 sc.

Rnd 3: (Sc in next 4 sc, 2 sc in next sc) twice: 12 sc.

Rnd 4: Sc in each sc around; slip st in next sc changing to Red, cut Lt Pink.

Rnd 5: Ch 1, sc in same st as slip st and in each sc around changing to White in last sc; do **not** join, place marker to indicated the beginning of the rnd; drop Red to **wrong** side of work.

Rnd 6: Sc in each sc around changing to Red in last sc; drop White to **wrong** side of work.

Rnd 7: Sc in each sc around changing to White in last sc; drop Red.

Rnds 8-11: Repeat Rnds 6 and 7 twice.

Rnd 12: (Sc2tog, sc in next 4 sc) twice changing to Red in last sc; cut White: 10 sc.

Stuff Arm with polyester fiberfill.

Joining Row: Ch 1; flatten top of Arm having ch at fold. Working through **both** loops of **both** pieces, sc in each st across; finish off leaving an 8" (20.5 cm) length for sewing.

Cap

BRIM

With White, ch 34; being careful **not** to twist ch, join with slip st to first ch to form a ring.

Rnd 1 (Right side)**:** Ch 1, sc in same ch as joining and in each ch around; join with slip st to first sc.

Note: Mark Rnd 1 as **right** side.

Rnd 2: Ch 1, sc in same st as joining and in each sc around; join with slip st to first sc, finish off.

BODY

Rnd 1: With **right** side facing and working in free loops of beginning ch, join Red with sc in first st; sc in each st around; join with slip st to first sc: 34 sc.

Note: Mark Rnd 1 as **right** side.

Rnd 2: Ch 1, sc in same st as joining, ★ sc2tog, sc in next 4 sc, sc2tog, sc in next 3 sc; repeat from ★ 2 times **more**; do **not** join, place marker to indicate the beginning of the rnd: 28 sc.

Rnd 3: (Sc2tog, sc in next 5 sc) around: 24 sc.

Rnd 4: Sc in each sc around.

Rnd 5: (Sc2tog, sc in next 4 sc) around: 20 sc.

Rnd 6: Sc in each sc around.

Rnd 7: (Sc2tog, sc in next 3 sc) around: 16 sc.

Rnd 8: Sc in each sc around.

Rnd 9: (Sc2tog, sc in next 2 sc) around: 12 sc.

Rnd 10: (Sc2tog, sc in next sc) around: 8 sc.

Rnd 11: Sc2tog around; slip st in next sc, finish off leaving a 6" (15 cm) length for sewing.

Thread yarn needle with end and weave through Front Loops Only of remaining sc to close; secure end.

Ear (Make 2)

Rnd 1 (Right side)**:** With Lt Pink, ch 2, 5 sc in second ch from hook; do **not** join.

Note: Mark Rnd 1 as **right** side.

Rnd 2: (Sc, hdc) in next sc, dc in next sc, ch 2, slip st in top of dc just made, hdc in same sc as dc, slip st in next sc; finish off leaving a 6" (15 cm) length for sewing.

Finishing

- Using Photo as a guide for placement and long ends:
- With Pink and using satin stitch ***(Fig. 6, page 27)***, add nose on Rnd 10.
- With a double strand of Black, add French knot eyes ***(Fig. 5, page 27)*** between Rnds 8 and 9.
- With Black, add an overcast stitch mouth on Rnd 12 ***(Fig. 8, page 27)***.
- With Gold, add turkey loop stitch hair to center of forehead on Rnd 5 and 6 of Head ***(Fig. 9, page 27)***.
- Sew Hat to head, covering the base of the Hair.
- Sew one Ear to each side of Head.
- Sew one Arm to each side of Body.
- Sew Legs to Body.
- With Gold and using straight stitch ***(Fig. 7, page 27)***, add buckle to Rnd 24.

Snowman

EASY

Finished Size: 8" (20.5 cm) tall

SHOPPING LIST

Yarn (Medium Weight) MEDIUM 4

- ☐ White - 62 yards (56.5 meters)
- ☐ Black - 38 yards (34.5 meters)
- ☐ Red - 10 yards (9 meters)
- ☐ Green - 2 yards (1.75 meters)
- ☐ Orange - small amount

Crochet Hook

- ☐ Size G (4 mm)
  or size needed for gauge

Additional Supplies

- ☐ Polyester fiberfill
- ☐ Yarn needle

GAUGE INFORMATION

8 sc and 8 rows/rnds = 2" (5 cm)

Gauge Swatch: 2" (5 cm) square

Ch 9.

Row 1: Sc in second ch from hook and in each ch across: 8 sc.

Rows 2-8: Ch 1, turn; sc in each sc across.

Finish off.

STITCH GUIDE

SINGLE CROCHET 2 TOGETHER *(abbreviated sc2tog)*

Pull up a loop in each of next 2 sc, YO and draw through all 3 loops on hook **(counts as one sc)**.

Head & Body

Rnd 1 (Right side)**:** With White, ch 2, 6 sc in second ch from hook; do **not** join, place marker to indicated the beginning of the rnd ***(see Markers, page 25)***.

Note: Loop a short piece of yarn around any stitch to mark Rnd 1 as **right** side.

Rnd 2: 2 Sc in each sc around: 12 sc.

Rnd 3: (2 Sc in next sc, sc in next sc) around: 18 sc.

Rnd 4: (2 Sc in next sc, sc in next 2 sc) around: 24 sc.

Rnd 5: (2 Sc in next sc, sc in next 3 sc) around: 30 sc.

Rnds 6-10: Sc in each sc around.

Rnd 11: (Sc2tog, sc in next 4 sc) around: 25 sc.

Rnd 12: Sc in each sc around.

Rnd 13: (Sc2tog, sc in next 3 sc) around: 20 sc.

Rnd 14: (Sc2tog, sc in next 2 sc) around: 15 sc.

Rnd 15: (Sc2tog, sc in next sc) around: 10 sc.

Stuff Head with polyester fiberfill.

Rnd 16: 2 Sc in each sc around: 20 sc.

Rnd 17: Sc in each sc around.

Rnd 18: (2 Sc in next sc, sc in next sc) around: 30 sc.

Rnds 19 and 20: Sc in each sc around.

Rnd 21: (2 Sc in next sc, sc in next 4 sc) around: 36 sc.

Rnd 22: Sc in each sc around.

Rnd 23: (2 Sc in next sc, sc in next 5 sc) around: 42 sc.

Rnds 24-28: Sc in each sc around.

Rnd 29: (Sc2tog, sc in next 4 sc) around: 35 sc.

Rnd 30: (Sc2tog, sc in next 3 sc) around: 28 sc.

Rnd 31: (Sc2tog, sc in next 2 sc) around: 21 sc.

Rnd 32: (Sc2tog, sc in next sc) around: 14 sc.

Stuff Body with polyester fiberfill.

Rnd 33: Sc2tog around; slip st in next sc, finish off leaving a 6" (15 cm) length for sewing.

Thread yarn needle with end and weave yarn through Front Loops Only of remaining sc ***(Fig. 2, page 26)***; secure end.

Boot & Leg (Make 2)

With Black, ch 5.

Rnd 1 (Right side)**:** Sc in second ch from hook and in next 2 chs, 5 sc in last ch; working in free loops of beginning ch ***(Fig. 3b, page 26)***, sc in next 2 chs, 2 sc in next ch; join with slip st to first sc: 12 sc.

Note: Mark Rnd 1 as **right** side.

Rnd 2: Ch 1, sc in same st as joining and in next 2 sc, 2 sc in next sc, sc in next sc, 3 sc in next sc, sc in next sc, 2 sc in next sc, sc in next 3 sc, 3 sc in last sc; join with slip st in first sc: 18 sc.

Rnd 3: Ch 1, sc in same st as joining and in next 3 sc, 2 sc in next sc, (sc in next sc, 2 sc in next sc) 3 times, sc in next 5 sc, 3 sc in next sc, sc in last sc; join with slip st to Back Loop Only of first sc ***(Fig. 2, page 26)***: 24 sc.

Rnd 4 (Sole ridge)**:** Ch 1, sc in same st as joining and in Back Loop Only of each sc around; join with slip st to **both** loops of first sc.

Rnd 5: Ch 1, sc in same st as joining and in both loops of each sc around; join with slip st to first sc.

Rnd 6: Ch 1, sc in same st as joining and in next 5 sc, sc2tog 5 times, sc in last 8 sc; join with slip st to first sc: 19 sc.

Rnd 7: Ch 1, sc in same st as joining and in next 4 sc, sc2tog 3 times, sc in last 8 sc; join with slip st to first sc: 16 sc.

Rnd 8: Ch 1, sc in same st as joining and in next 4 sc, sc2tog twice, sc in last 7 sc; join with slip st to first sc changing to White ***(Fig. 4a, page 26)***; cut Black: 14 sc.

Rnd 9: Ch 1, sc in same st as joining and in each sc around; join with slip st to first sc.

Stuff Foot with polyester fiberfill.

Rnds 10 and 11: Ch 1, sc in same st as joining and in each sc around; join with slip st to first sc; at end of Rnd 11, finish off leaving a 10" (25.5 cm) length for sewing.

Stuff Leg firmly with polyester fiberfill.

Mitt & Arm (Make 2)

Rnd 1 (Right side)**:** With Red, ch 2; 5 sc in second ch from hook; do **not** join, place marker to indicate the beginning of the rnd.

Note: Mark Rnd 1 as **right** side.

Rnd 2: 2 Sc in each sc around: 10 sc.

Rnd 3: (Sc in next 4 sc, 2 sc in next sc) twice: 12 sc.

Rnds 4 and 5: Sc in each sc around; at end of Rnd 5, slip st in next sc, finish off.

Rnd 6: With **right** side facing, join White with sc in same st as slip st ***(see Joining With Sc, page 25)***; sc in each sc around; join with slip st to first sc.

Rnd 7: Ch 1, sc in same st as joining and in each sc around; do **not** join, place marker to indicate the beginning of the rnd.

Rnds 8-10: Sc in each sc around.

Rnd 11: (Sc2tog, sc in next 4 sc) twice: 10 sc.

Stuff Arm with polyester fiberfill.

Joining Row: Ch 1; flatten top of Arm having ch at fold. Working through **both** loops of **both** pieces, sc in each st across; finish off leaving an 8" (20.5 cm) length for sewing.

Hat

Rnd 1 (Right side)**:** With Black, ch 2, 6 sc in second ch from hook; do **not** join, place marker to indicated the beginning of the rnd.

Note: Mark Rnd 1 as **right** side.

Rnd 2: 2 Sc in each sc around: 12 sc.

Rnd 3: (2 Sc in next sc, sc in next sc) around: 18 sc.

Rnd 4: (2 Sc in next sc, sc in next 2 sc) around: 24 sc.

Rnd 5: (2 Sc in next sc, sc in next 3 sc) around: 30 sc.

Rnd 6 (Turning ridge)**:** Working in Back Loops Only, (slip st, ch 1, sc) in next sc, sc in each sc around, remove marker; join with slip st to **both** loops of first sc.

Rnd 7: Ch 1, sc in same st as joining and in both loops of each sc around; do **not** join, place marker to indicate the beginning of the rnd.

Rnd 8: (Sc in next 4 sc, sc2tog) around: 25 sc.

Rnd 9: Sc in each sc around.

Rnd 10: (Sc in next 4 sc, 2 sc in next sc) around: 30 sc.

Rnd 11 (Brim turning ridge)**:** Working in Front Loops Only, (sc in next 2 sc, 2 sc in next sc) around: 40 sc.

Rnd 12: Working in both loops, (hdc in next sc, 2 hdc in next sc, sc in next 2 sc) around; slip st in next hdc, finish off: 50 sts.

Scarf

Bottom Edge: With Red and leaving a 3" (7.5 cm) length for fringe, ch 41; finish off leaving a 3" (7.5 cm) length for fringe.

Row 1 (Right side)**:** Leaving a 3" (7.5 cm) length for fringe and working in back ridge of chs ***(Fig. A)***, join Green with sc in first ch of Bottom Edge; ★ ch 1, skip next ch, sc in next ch; repeat from ★ across; finish off leaving a 3" (7.5 cm) length for fringe: 21 sc and 20 ch-1 sps.

Fig. A

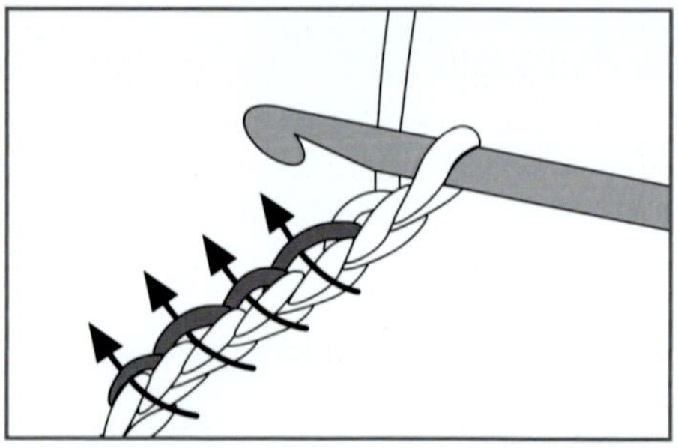

Note: Mark Row 1 as **right** side.

Top Edge: Leaving a 3" (7.5 cm) length for fringe, join Red with sc in first sc of Row 1; (sc in next ch-1 sp, ch 1) across to last ch-1 sp, sc in last ch-1 sp and in last sc; finish off leaving a 3" (7.5 cm) length for fringe.

Button (Make 2)

With Black, make an adjustable ring and work 5 sc in ring ***(Figs. 1a-d, page 25)***; join with slip st to first sc; finish off leaving a 6" (15 cm) length for sewing.

Nose

With Orange, ch 4; slip st in second ch from hook, sc in last 2 chs; finish off leaving a 6" length for sewing.

Finishing

Using Photo as a guide for placement and long ends:

- Using satin stitch ***(Fig. 6, page 27)***, add Black eyes over Rnds 7 and 8, leaving 3 stitches between eyes.
- Sew Nose to center of face between Rnds 9 and 10.
- Sew one Arm to each side of Body.
- Sew Legs to Body.
- Sew Buttons to center of Body.
- Add 3 French knots along brim turning ridge of Hat ***(Fig. 5, page 27)***; then sew Hat to Head.
- Using two, 3" (7.5 cm) strands of Red yarn and one 3" (7.5 cm) strand of Green yarn, add fringe to each end of Scarf ***(Figs. B & C)***; wrap Scarf around Neck and tack in place.

Fringe

Fold strands in half. With wrong side facing and using crochet hook, draw the folded end up through end of row and pull the loose ends through the folded end ***(Fig. B)***; draw the knot up tightly ***(Fig. C)***. Repeat in end of each row. Trim ends evenly.

Fig. B

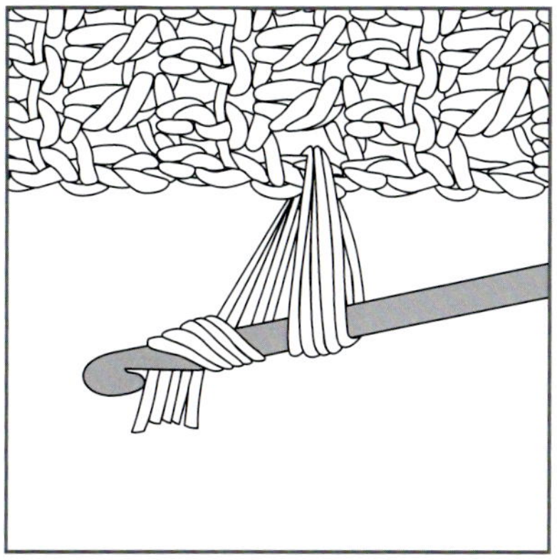

Fig. C

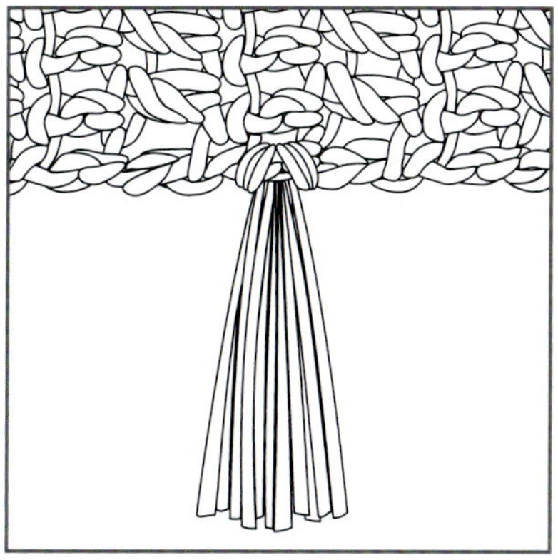

GENERAL INSTRUCTIONS

Abbreviations

ch(s)	chain(s)
cm	centimeters
dc	double crochet(s)
hdc	half double crochet(s)
mm	millimeters
Rnd(s)	Round(s)
sc	single crochet(s)
sc2tog	single crochet 2 together
sp(s)	space(s)
st(s)	stitch(es)
YO	yarn over

Symbols & Terms

★ — work instructions following ★ as many **more** times as indicated in addition to the first time.

( ) or **[ ]** — work enclosed instructions **as many** times as specified by the number immediately following **or** work all enclosed instructions in the stitch or space indicated **or** contains explanatory remarks.

colon (:) — the number(s) given after a colon at the end of a row or round denote(s) the number of stitches you should have on that row or round.

Gauge

Exact gauge is **essential** for proper size. Before beginning your project, make the sample swatch given in the instructions in the yarn and hook specified. After completing the swatch, measure it, counting your stitches and rows or rounds carefully. If your swatch is larger or smaller than specified, **make another, changing hook size to get the correct gauge.** Keep trying until you find the size hook that will give you the specified gauge.

CROCHET TERMINOLOGY		
UNITED STATES		INTERNATIONAL
slip stitch (slip st)	=	single crochet (sc)
single crochet (sc)	=	double crochet (dc)
half double crochet (hdc)	=	half treble crochet (htr)
double crochet (dc)	=	treble crochet (tr)
treble crochet (tr)	=	double treble crochet (dtr)
double treble crochet (dtr)	=	triple treble crochet (ttr)
triple treble crochet (tr tr)	=	quadruple treble crochet (qtr)
skip	=	miss

BASIC	Projects using basic stitches. May include basic increases and decreases.
EASY	Projects may include simple stitch patterns, color work, and/or shaping.
INTERMEDIATE	Projects may include involved stitch patterns, color work, and/or shaping.
COMPLEX	Projects may include complex stitch patterns, color work, and/or shaping using a variety of techniques and stitches simultaneously.

CROCHET HOOKS																
U.S.	B-1	C-2	D-3	E-4	F-5	G-6	7	H-8	I-9	J-10	K-10½	L-11	M/N-13	N/P-15	P/Q	Q	S
Metric - mm	2.25	2.75	3.25	3.5	3.75	4	4.5	5	5.5	6	6.5	8	9	10	15	16	19

Markers

Markers are used to help distinguish the beginning of each round being worked. Place a 2" (5 cm) scrap piece of yarn before the first stitch of each round, moving marker after each round is complete.

Joining With Sc

When instructed to join with sc, begin with a slip knot on the hook. Insert hook in stitch indicated, YO and pull up a loop, YO and draw through both loops on hook.

Adjustable Loop

Wind the yarn around two fingers to form a ring ***(Fig. 1a)***, slide the yarn off your fingers and grasp the strands at the top of the ring ***(Fig. 1b)***. Insert the hook from **front** to **back** into the ring, pull up a loop, YO and draw through the loop on hook to lock the ring ***(Fig. 1c)***. Working around **both** strands, work stitches in the ring as specified, then pull the yarn end to close ***(Fig. 1d)***.

Fig. 1a

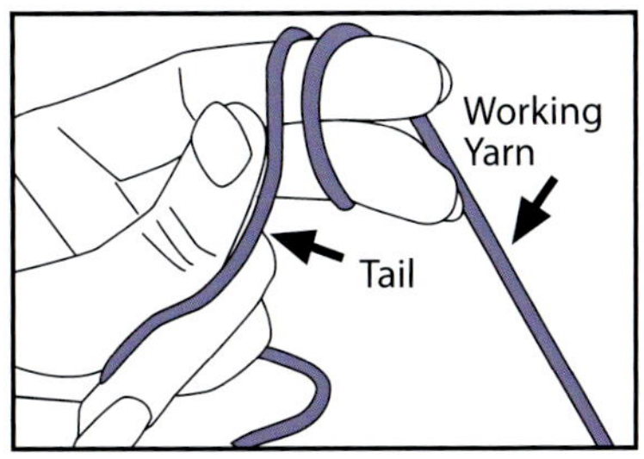

Fig. 1b

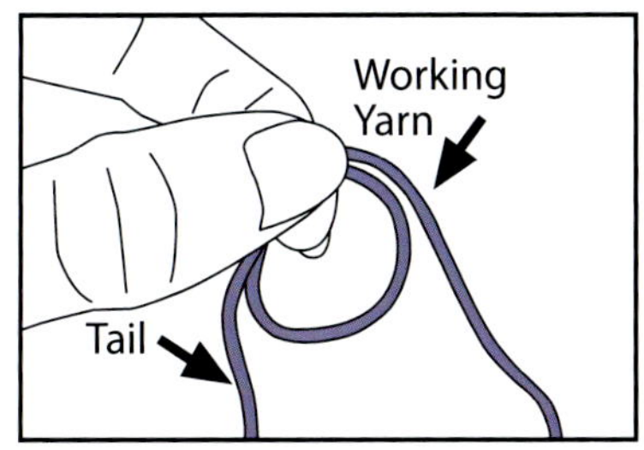

Fig. 1c

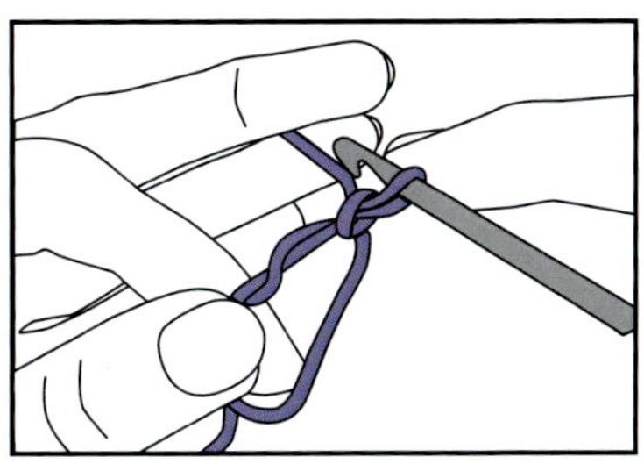

Fig. 1d

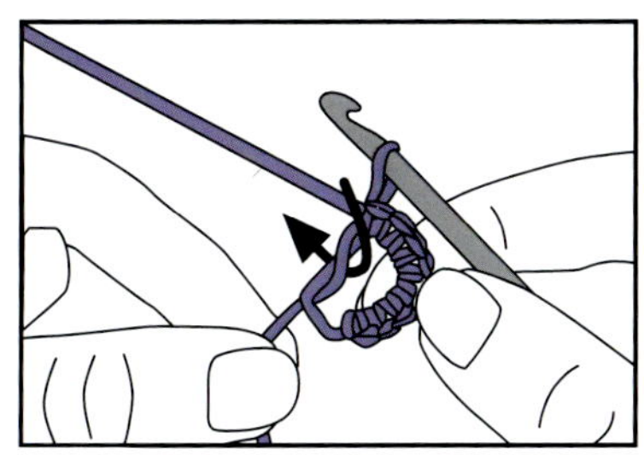

Yarn Weight Symbol & Names	LACE 0	SUPER FINE 1	FINE 2	LIGHT 3	MEDIUM 4	BULKY 5	SUPER BULKY 6	JUMBO 7
Type of Yarns in Category	Fingering, size 10 crochet thread	Sock, Fingering, Baby	Sport, Baby	DK, Light Worsted	Worsted, Afghan, Aran	Chunky, Craft, Rug	Super Bulky, Roving	Jumbo, Roving
Crochet Gauge* Ranges in Single Crochet to 4" (10 cm)	32-42 sts**	21-32 sts	16-20 sts	12-17 sts	11-14 sts	8-11 sts	6-9 sts	5 sts and fewer
Advised Hook Size Range	Steel*** 6 to 8, Regular hook B-1	B-1 to E-4	E-4 to 7	7 to I-9	I-9 to K-10½	K-10½ to M/N-13	M/N-13 to Q	Q and larger

*GUIDELINES ONLY: The chart above reflects the most commonly used gauges and hook sizes for specific yarn categories.

** Lace weight yarns are usually crocheted with larger hooks to create lacy openwork patterns. Accordingly, a gauge range is difficult to determine. Always follow the gauge stated in your pattern.

*** Steel crochet hooks are sized differently from regular hooks–the higher the number, the smaller the hook, which is the reverse of regular hook sizing.

Back Or Front Loops Only

Work only in loop(s) indicated by arrow *(Fig. 2)*.

Fig. 2

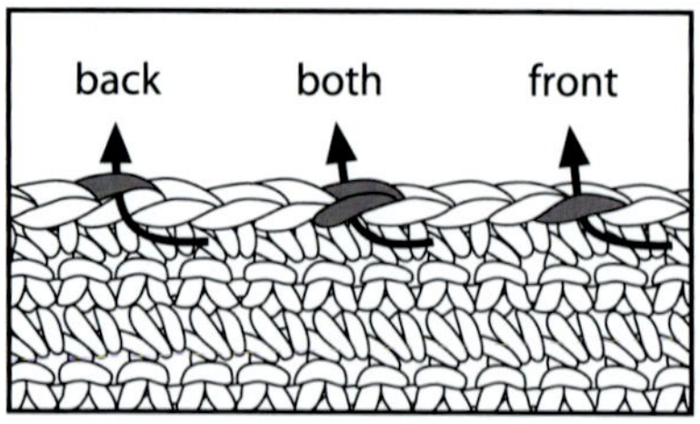

Free Loops

After working in Back of Front Loops Only on a row or round, there will be a ridge of unused loops. These are called the free loops. Later, when instructed to work in the free loops of the same row or round, work in these loops *(Fig. 3a)*.

When instructed to work in free loops of a chain, work in loop indicated by arrow *(Fig. 3b)*.

Fig. 3a

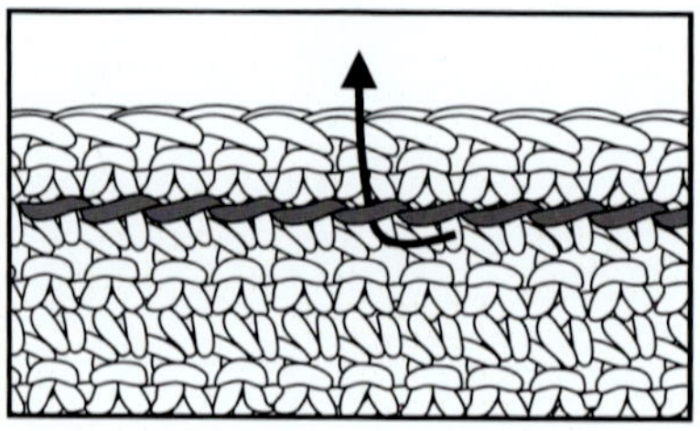

Fig. 3b

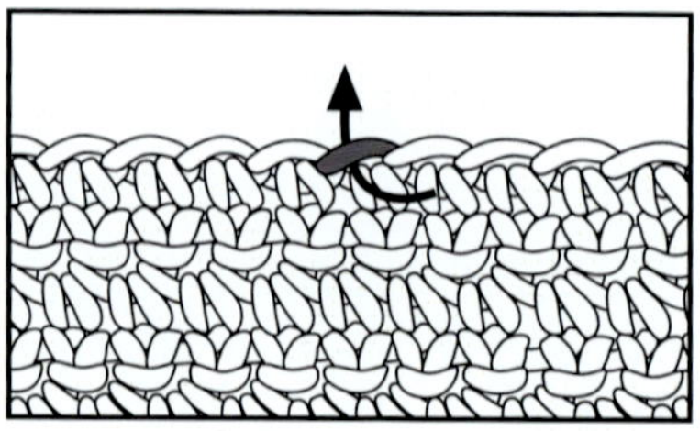

Changing Colors

Work the last stitch to within one step of completion hook new yarn ***(Figs. 4a & 4b)*** and draw through all loops on hook. Do **not** cut old color unless otherwise indicated.

Fig. 4a

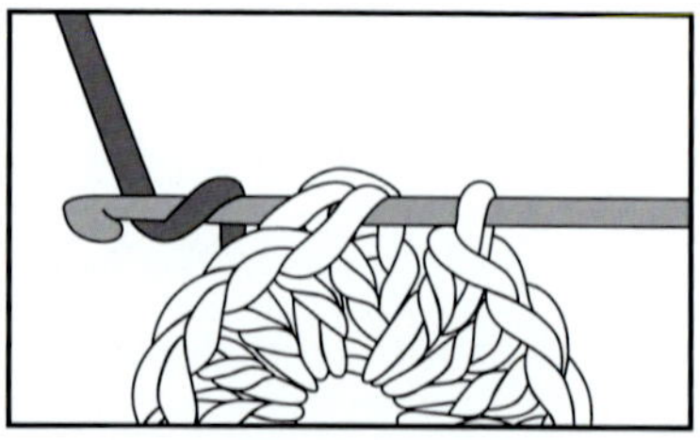

Fig. 4b

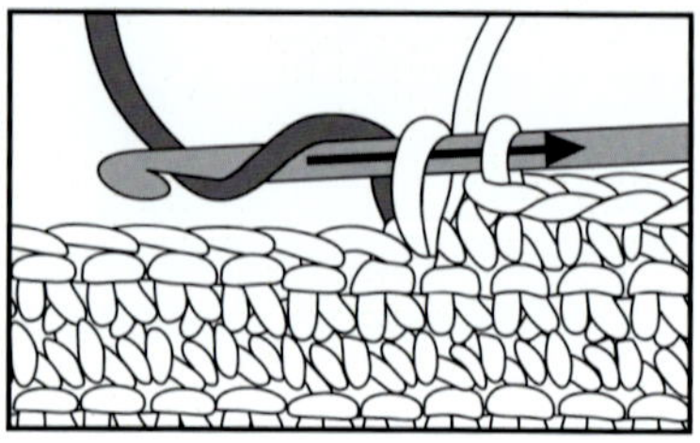

Embroidery Stitches

FRENCH KNOT

Bring needle up at 1. Wrap yarn around the needle once and insert the needle at 2, holding end of yarn with non-stitching fingers ***(Fig. 5)***. Tighten knot; then pull needle through, holding yarn until it must be released.

Fig. 5

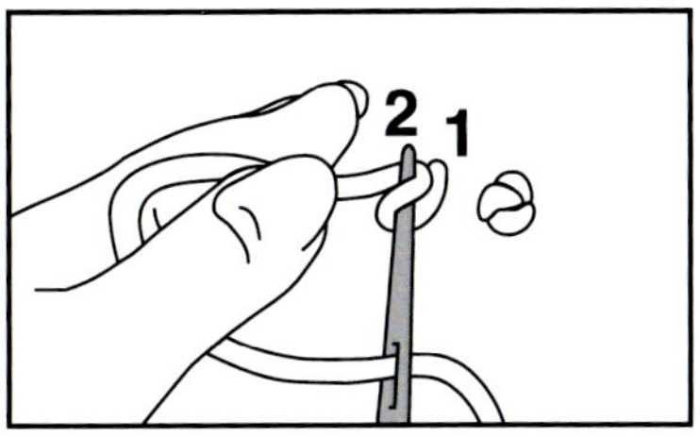

SATIN STITCH

Satin stitch is a series of straight stitches entering and exiting the same hole or worked side-by-side. Bring the needle up at 1 and go down at 2 ***(Fig. 6)***.

Fig. 6

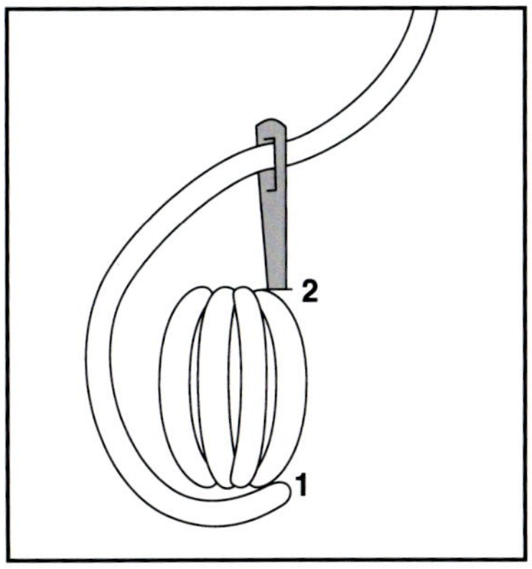

STRAIGHT STITCH

Straight stitch is just what the name implies, a single, straight stitch. Come up at 1 and go down at 2 ***(Fig. 7)***.

Fig. 7

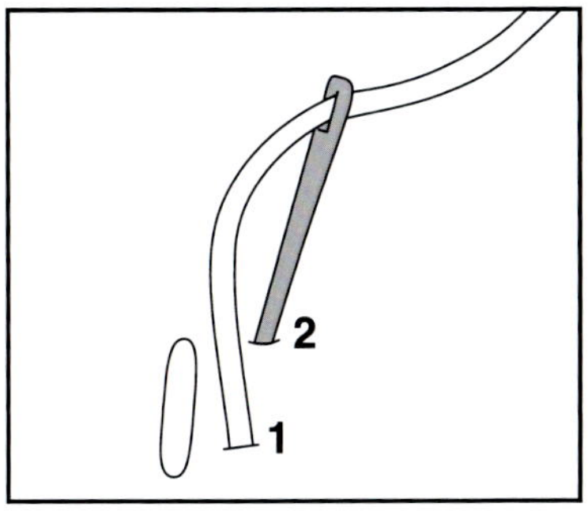

OVERCAST STITCH

An overcast stitch is used to form a curved line from a straight stitch, holding it in place. Come up at 1, go down at 2 ***(Fig. 8)***.

Fig. 8

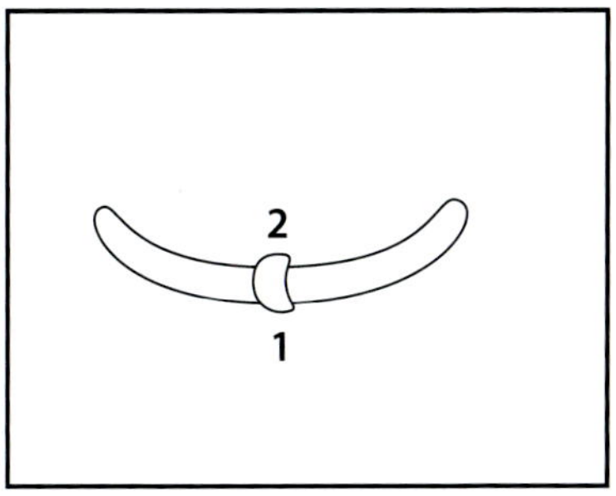

TURKEY LOOP STITCH

Bring the needle up at 1 and go down at 2 leaving a ¾" (1.9 cm) loop ***(Fig. 9a)***, come up at 3 and go down at 4 to secure loop ***(Fig. 9b)***. Repeat for each loop ***(Fig. 9c)***.

Fig. 9a

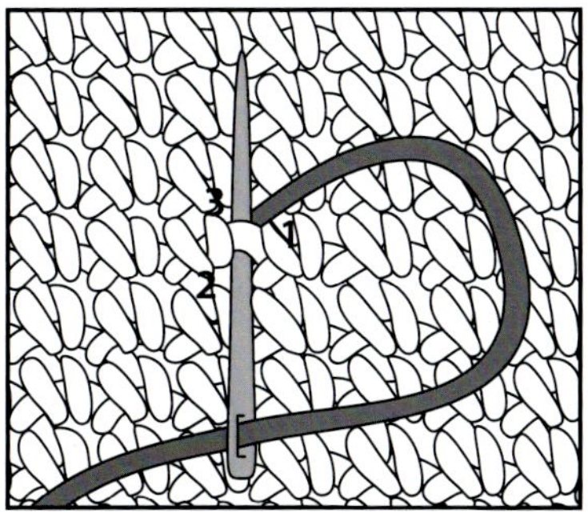

Fig. 9b

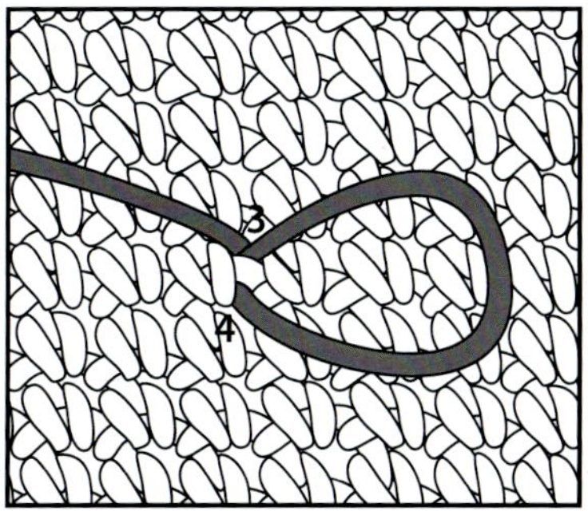

Fig. 9c

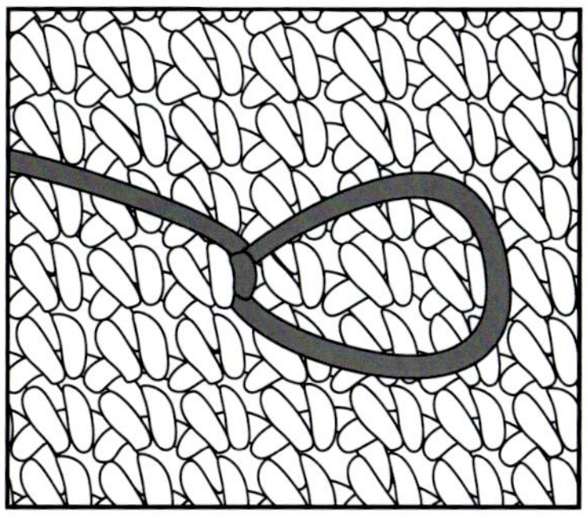

YARN INFORMATION

The projects in this book were made using Medium Weight Yarn. Any brand of medium weight yarn may be used. It is best to refer to the yardage/meters when determining how many balls or skeins to purchase. Remember, to arrive at the finished size, it is the GAUGE/TENSION that is important, not the brand of yarn.

For your convenience, listed below are the specific yarns used to create our photography models. Because yarn manufacturers make frequent changes to their product lines, you may sometimes find it necessary to use a substitute yarn or to search for the discontinued product at alternate suppliers (locally or online).

SANTA
Lion Brand® Vanna's Choice®
Red - #113 Scarlet
White - #100 White
Black - #153 Black
Green - #172 Kelly Green
Red Heart® Amore™
Lt. Pink - #6724 Peaceful

MRS. CLAUS
Lion Brand® Vanna's Choice®
Red - #113 Scarlet
White - #100 White
Black - #153 Black
Green - #172 Kelly Green
Red Heart® Amore™
Lt. Pink - #6724 Peaceful

ELF
Red Heart® Soft®
Bright Green - #4420 Guacamole
Lion Brand® Vanna's Choice®
Red - #113 Scarlet
White - #100 White
Black - #153 Black
Gold - #158 Mustard
Red Heart® Amore™
Lt. Pink - #6724 Peaceful

SNOWMAN
Lion Brand® Vanna's Choice®
White - #100 White
Black - #153 Black
Red - #113 Scarlet
Green - #172 Kelly Green
Orange scrap yarn

Made in U.S.A.